A Passover Seder Script

FOR CHRISTIAN FAMILIES

LYNDA CHERRY

ISBN 13: 978-1-4621-4590-4

Published by CFI, an imprint of Cedar Fort, Inc.
2373 W. 700 S., Suite 100, Springville, UT 84663
Distributed by Cedar Fort, Inc., www.cedarfort.com

Cover design by Courtney Proby

Typeset by Kyle Lund

Printed in the United States of America

10 9 8 7 6 5 4 3 2 1

Printed on acid-free paper

Contents

Introduction

There are more than 2,000 different Passover Seder texts. They continue to evolve and to change to fit the desires of those who celebrate it.

This script was written with the desire to follow a text that would most closely fit that which the Savior and His apostles might have used during the last Passover feast He kept with them, a Passover whose sacred emblems He identified as pertaining to Himself. On that hallowed evening, He used bread and wine, symbols long revered in the ritual, to introduce a new covenant: the sacrament of His flesh and blood.

The Passover Seder text is derived from the *Haggadah,* the oral "story" passed down from generation to generation. In fact, the Seder can perhaps best be described as a "talk-feast." This talk-feast was the manner in which the story of Israel's salvation and birth as a nation was passed from one generation to the next. Long before printed books and formal schools, the yearly Seder night transformed every Jewish home into a classroom, with the *Haggadah* (from the Hebrew root 'to tell') as the text.

"The word 'Seder' means order. The tradition understands the Passover table ritual as a fixed progression, 15 steps, a logical unfolding of the single most important Jewish lesson from the retelling of the single most significant Jewish experience. The Pesach Seder is a talk-feast in four acts" (http://tiwestport.org/passover/outline.html).

The word "Seder" was not used at the time of Christ, therefore, we will forgo its usage in the following text, and refer to the feast by the name by which it was called for millennia: simply "The Passover", or "*Pesach*" (Hebrew).

Because the *Haggadah* source is oral, many variations have worked their way into the story. To demonstrate the variety and adaptability of the Passover text, some of the variances include, but are not limited to:

- Eating lamb.
- Not eating lamb because:

  (1) The temple is no longer in use, thereby sacrifices cannot be made,

  or

  (2) Christians look to the lamb as a symbol of Christ, and Jews look at Christians as persecutors (http://www.godonthe.net/passover/faq.html).
- All attendees participate in the reading.
- One "elder" recites the entire event, chanting in the traditional Hebrew method.
- Keeping Passover because one is a Jew and believes the Passover is one of the traditions that sets him apart as one of God's chosen people.
- Keeping Passover because one is a Jew, and wants to be set apart in terms of ethnicity, but does not recite the deliverance from Egypt as being performed by God, or refer to any religious aspects during the ceremony. One modern source states: "None of this requires a set of beliefs. Indeed, Jews have no specific dogma, only a set of customs. Being Jewish, wanting to participate in the ritual of the Seder, does not necessarily require any kind of religious belief" (Ira Steingroot, *Keeping Passover*, p. 8).

The Passover script that follows is a compilation from many sources. Those sources will be listed at the end of the text, but will not necessarily be footnoted as they appear.

The goal in creating the following text is to help place and identify the significance of Jesus' atoning sacrifice within the context of the Passover Feast, particularly as it applied to the last events of His mortal life. Reading in this light helps us to understand the symbols and recitations with greater clarity and pertinence: the Passover *is* the testament of His life and mission. "And behold, this is the whole meaning of the law, every whit pointing to that great and last sacrifice; and that great and last sacrifice will be the Son of God, yea infinite and eternal" (Alma 34:14).

Lastly, many ask what Jews think of Christians participating in the Passover Seder event. It depends upon *which* Jew you are asking. Some find it an offense, but others express a feeling of being honored by the remembrance. Certainly all would agree that it makes a difference as to how the occasion is approached; if it is undertaken in an attitude of play-acting or mere curiosity it may be thought offensive. However, if approached in an attitude of sincere reverence and worship of the God of Israel, recognizing His power over the whole earth, no fault can be found. **Furthermore, the commandment given by God to keep the Passover was given to "the children of Israel" – not to the Jewish people alone, and it is called *the Lord's* Passover** (Lev. 23:2-5; Num. 9:1-4). To remove any further doubt on the subject, the Lord commanded: "And if a stranger shall sojourn among you, and will keep the passover unto the LORD; according to the ordinance of the passover, and according to the manner thereof, so shall he do: ye shall have one ordinance, both for the stranger, and for him that was born in the land" (Num. 9:14).

The First Passover

And the LORD spake unto Moses and Aaron in the land of Egypt, saying, This month shall be unto you the beginning of months: it shall be the first month of the year to you.

Speak ye unto all the congregation of Israel, saying, In the tenth day of this month they shall take to them every man a lamb, according to the house of their fathers; a lamb for an house. . . Your lamb shall be without blemish, a male of the first year: ye shall take it out from the sheep, or from the goats: And ye shall keep it up until the fourteenth day of the same month: and the whole assembly of the congregation of Israel shall kill it in the evening.

And they shall take of the blood, and strike it on the two side posts and on the upper door post of the houses, wherein they shall eat it. And they shall eat the flesh in that night, roast with fire, and unleavened bread; and with bitter herbs they shall eat it. Eat not of it raw, nor sodden at all with water, but roast with fire; his head with his legs, and with the purtenance thereof. And ye shall let nothing of it remain until the morning; and that which remaineth of it until the morning ye shall burn with fire.

And thus shall ye eat it; with your loins girded, your shoes on your feet, and your staff in your hand; and ye shall eat it in haste: it is the LORD'S passover.

For I will pass through the land of Egypt this night, and will smite all the firstborn in the land of Egypt, both man and beast; and against all the gods of Egypt will I execute judgment: I am the LORD.

And the blood shall be to you for a token upon the houses where ye are: and when I see the blood, I will pass over you, and the plague shall not be upon you to destroy you, when I smite the land of Egypt.

And this day shall be unto you for a memorial; and ye shall keep it a feast to the LORD throughout your generations; ye shall keep it a feast by an ordinance forever.

Seven days shall ye eat unleavened bread; even the first day ye shall put away leaven out of your houses: for whosoever eateth leavened bread from the first day until the seventh day, that soul shall be cut off from Israel.

And in the first day there shall be an holy convocation, and in the seventh day there shall be an holy convocation to you; no manner of work shall be done in them, save that which man must eat, that only may be done of you.

And ye shall observe the feast of unleavened bread; for in this selfsame day have I brought your armies out of the land of Egypt: therefore shall ye observe this day in your generations by an ordinance forever (Exodus 12:1-14).

Commandment to Keep the Passover

And the LORD spake unto Moses, saying, Speak unto the children of Israel, and say unto them, Concerning the feasts of the LORD, which ye shall proclaim to be holy convocations, even these are my feasts. ... In the fourteenth day of the first month at even is the LORD's Passover. And on the fifteenth day of the same month is the feast of unleavened bread unto the LORD: seven days ye must eat unleavened bread. In the first day ye shall have an holy convocation: ye shall do no servile work therein. But ye shall offer an offering made by fire unto the Lord seven days: in the seventh day is an holy convocation: ye shall do no servile work therein (Lev. 23: 1-8).

Three times in a year shall all thy males appear before the LORD thy God in the place which he shall choose; in the feast of unleavened bread, and in the feast of weeks, and in the feast of tabernacles: and they shall not appear before the LORD empty (Deut. 16:16).

Alterations to the First Passover

The first Passover differed somewhat from those succeeding it. Three great changes or developments were made almost immediately in the nature of the Feast of the Passover: (1) It lost its domestic character, and became a sanctuary (or temple) feast. 2) A seven days' feast of unleavened bread (hence its usual name), with special offerings was added (Ex. 12:15; Num. 28:16-25). The first and seventh days were Sabbaths and days of holy convocation. (3) The feast was connected with the harvest. On the morrow after the Sabbath (= 16th Abib probably) a sheaf of the first fruits of the harvest (barley) was waved before the Lord (Lev. 23:10-14).

In later times the following ceremonies were added: (1) the history of the redemption from Egypt was related by the head of the household (cf. Ex. 12:26-27). (2) Four cups of wine mixed with water were drunk at different stages of the feast (cf. Luke 22:17, 20; 1 Cor. 10:16, the cup of blessing). (3) Psalms 113-118 (the *Hallel*) were sung. (4) The various materials of the feast were dipped in a sauce. (5) The feast was not eaten standing, but reclining. (6) The Levites (at least on some occasions) slew the sacrifices. (7) Voluntary peace offerings (called *Chagigah*) were offered. Of these there are traces in the law and in the history (Num. 10:10; 2 Chr. 30:22-24; 35:13). (8) A second Passover for those prevented by ceremonial uncleanness from keeping the Passover at the proper time was instituted by Moses (Num. 9:10) on the 14th day of the second month. This was called the Little Passover (*Bible Dictionary*, "Feasts," p. 672).

Remarkable Passover Celebrations

- With Moses in the Sinai wilderness (Num. 9:4).
- With Joshua before taking Jericho. The manna from heaven ceased the day after this Passover. Before they could participate in the Passover, the males had to be circumcised, as none had been circumcised since they had left Egypt (Josh. 5:3-12).
- Under King Hezekiah after he cleansed the land of idols; he invited all of Israel to come and celebrate the Passover, for it had not been held for many years. Because the Levites were not clean at the time the Passover should have been held, they held it on the second month. The people rejoiced so much in the spiritual healing that occurred that they all agreed to keep the Passover for an additional seven days, for a total of two weeks (2 Chr. 30).
- Under King Josiah after he had cleansed the land of idols, and the book of the Law was found in the Temple and read to the people: "Surely there was not holden such a passover from the days of the judges that judged Israel, nor in all the days of the kings of Israel, nor of the kings of Judah" (2 Kings 23:21; 2 Chr. 35).
- Following the completion of the second temple built after the return of the Jews from Babylon (Ezra 6:15-20).
- With Jesus and His disciples (Matt. 26:2, 17-19; Luke 22; John 13-14).
- Ezekiel's vision of a future Passover held following the building and dedication of the latter-day temple in Jerusalem (Ezek. 45:21).

When Is Passover?

Passover is celebrated on the 14th of Abib, or Nisan, usually corresponding to the month of April. It is a time of full moon. The Feast technically lasts from sundown of the 14th until sundown of the 15th, but may be celebrated as early as noon on the 14th. (The day after Passover begins the seven-day Feast of Unleavened Bread.) The importance of the Passover is emphasized by the fact that it is the day of the new year according to the law given to Moses.

Instructions

This script is meant to be used as a companion to the book "The Feasts and Festivals of the Messiah," by Lynda Cherry.

This script offers a foundation from which to build your own "talk-feast," that can be enriched by sharing your own insights and feelings throughout the Passover feast. The full script, with discussion and meal, typically lasts 3-4 hours.

Many parts are to be read aloud and have been organized into numbered parts that should be shared between many readers. Parts of the dinner needing to be performed have been outlined as Instructions.

Preparations

- Bowls of saltwater to accommodate up to six guests each.
- Karpas (parsley or similar) cut in pieces and arranged on plates.
- Finger bowls with lemon slices for finger washing of up to four guests each.
- Bitter herbs (horseradish) for easy sharing.
- Unleavened bread in baskets — set aside 3 whole pieces and white linen napkins to wrap them.

- Charoseth (an apple mixture representing mortar, the recipe is easily found on many websites).
- Grape juice (winc) for four cups for each guest.
- Candles to light at the beginning of the feast.
- Passover meal per taste and interest of the assembly. This can include traditional lamb, potatoes, green beans, etc. following Kosher rules.

PROLOGUE

Remove All Leaven
Performed by the Head of the Household

Reader #1: On the previous night the head of the household searched his home using a lighted candle, and a feather, looking for any leaven that may have been missed in the general cleaning and preparations. All leaven is to be removed and destroyed.

"Blessed art Thou, Jehovah, our God, King of the Universe, who hast sanctified us by Thy commandments, and commanded us to remove the leaven."

The search itself was to be accomplished in perfect silence.

Reader #2: Commentary: The analogy is made of sin to yeast, as sin tends to corrupt and spoil the soul. Also, many are "puffed up" in the sin of pride. Jesus warned to "beware the leaven of the Pharisees and Sadduccees" (Matt. 16:6).

Scriptural Commentary: 1 Cor. 5:6-8 "Your glorying is not good. Know ye not that a little leaven leaveneth the whole lump? Purge out therefore the old leaven, that ye may be a new lump, as ye are unleavened. For even Christ our passover is sacrificed for us: Therefore let us keep the feast, not with old leaven, neither with the leaven of malice and wickedness; but with the unleavened bread of sincerity and truth."

Speaking of His Second Coming, the Lord warns: "And it shall come to pass at that time that I will search Jerusalem with candles, and punish the men that are settled on their lees (complacent or indifferent): that say in their heart, The LORD will not do good, neither will he do evil" (Zephaniah 1:12).

Question and

Discussion: What is the significance of the head of the household having this role of searching for hidden leaven?

Would Jesus have found any "spiritual leaven" in His search the night He kept the last Passover with His apostles?

Lighting of the Candles

Instructions: Today, the Festival Lights are lit by a woman. She lights the candles (do so now), and recites:

Reader #3: "The LORD bless thee, and keep thee: the LORD make his face shine upon thee, and be gracious unto thee: The LORD lift up his countenance upon thee, and give thee peace" (Numbers 6:24-26).

Scriptural Commentary: "Then spake Jesus again unto them, saying, I am the light of the world: he that followeth me shall not walk in darkness, but shall have the light of life" (John 8:12).

"I am come a light into the world, that whosoever believeth on me should not abide in darkness" (John 12:46).

Jesus and His Apostles

Reader #4: Scriptural Commentary: Jesus had said: "Ye know that after two days is the feast of the passover, and the Son of man is betrayed to be crucified" (Matthew 26:2).

"Now, before the feast of the passover, when Jesus knew that his hour was come that he should depart out of this world unto the Father, having loved his own which were in the world, he loved them unto the end" (John 13:1).

"Then came the day of unleavened bread, when the passover must be killed. And he sent Peter and John, saying, Go and prepare us the passover that we may eat.

"And they said unto him, Where wilt thou that we prepare? And he said unto them, Behold, when ye are entered into the city, there shall a man meet you, bearing a pitcher of water; follow him into the house where he entereth in. And ye shall say unto the Goodman of the house, The Master saith unto thee, Where is the guestchamber, where I shall eat the passover with my disciples?

"And he shall shew you a large upper room furnished: there make ready.

"And they went, and found as he had said unto them: and they made ready the passover.

"And when the hour was come, he sat down, and the twelve apostles with him.

"And he said unto them, With desire I have desired to eat this passover with you before I suffer: For I say unto you, I will not any more eat thereof, until it be fulfilled which is written in the prophets concerning me. Then I will partake with you, in the kingdom of God" (Luke 22:7-15 &16 with JST footnote).

"Judas had already entered into an agreement with the chief priests to betray Jesus into their hands, so that they "might kill him" (Mark 14:10-11; Luke 22:2). He had received thirty pieces of silver, the price of a slave, for his betrayal. The money was paid to him out of the temple-treasury.

Reader #5: Commentary: "We mark the deep symbolic significance of it all, in that the Lord was, so to speak, paid for out of the temple-money which was destined for the purchase of sacrifices, and that He, Who took on Him the form of a servant, was sold and bought at the legal price of a slave" (Edersheim, *The Life and Times of Jesus the Messiah*, 2:477).

"In Jesus' day … the Rabbinic decree then was that all who ate should recline at a table, to indicate rest, safety, and liberty. It was the custom for each person to occupy a separate divan or pillow, to lie on his left side and lean on his left hand, the feet stretching back towards the ground.

"It is interesting, based on the scriptural allusions and inferences, to place Jesus and at least three of the Twelve in the positions they may have occupied at the table. As the Twelve began to take selected positions at the table, a contention arose, evidently over precedence of seating (Luke 22:24). By instinct we feel Judas – who was out of harmony with his brethren – was at the root of the trouble. Among the Pharisees this matter of rank and precedence, of what place each person occupied at the table, was a matter of great concern; and Judas – influenced by the prince of this world, who is Lucifer – was more of a Pharisee than a Christian. He, by training and inclination, would follow the Pharisaic custom and seek for himself the seat of honor.

"With whom would he contend? Obviously with Peter, who was in fact the chief apostle and who knew his place was at the Lord's side in the position of honor and precedence. When Jesus rebuked the contention, a very natural thing would happen: impetuous Peter would go and take the lowest seat, while spiritually hardened Judas, immune to feelings of conscience and decency, would maintain his claim and take the seat of honor at the side of Jesus. This suggests the position of two of the Twelve.

"As to the Beloved John, he leaned on the Master's bosom, which could only be done if he were on Jesus' right side. It was the custom for the chief personage at a feast to have someone on either side. Thus, starting on one side of the table, we would have John, then Jesus, and then Judas; the others would place themselves where they chose, but Peter would go across from John at the foot of the table. Thus when Christ told John the sign by which the traitor would be known, none of the others would hear him. Thus Jesus, as part of the Paschal ceremony, could give the sop first to Judas, who sat in the seat of honor at his left hand. Thus when Judas asked if his treachery was known, and received an affirmative answer, none of the others knew what was involved. And thus Peter, having placed himself at the foot, would have to beckon to John to ask who it was who should betray the Lord (John 13:23-27)" (McConkie, *The Mortal Messiah*, 4:31-32).

THE FEAST BEGINS

Instructions: Do not drink or eat until instructed to do so. There are many occasions when all present will hold up "the cup" but not drink.

Reader #1: There are "four cups" of wine (grape juice). Each has its own title, and prayer associated with it. The titles of the cups are taken from Exodus 6:6-7: "Wherefore say unto the children of Israel, I am the LORD, and I will bring you out from under the burdens of the Egyptians, and I will rid you of their bondage, and I will redeem you with a stretched out arm, and with great judgments: And I will take you to me for a people, and I will be to you a God: and ye shall know that I am the LORD your God, which bringeth you out from under the burdens of the Egyptians."

The titles, accordingly are:

1) I Will Bring You Out,

2) I Will Deliver You,

3) I Will Redeem You, and

4) I Will Take You to Me.

Instructions: When each cup is filled, it must be drunk completely when instructed. Keep this in mind when filling the cups.

The First Cup — (Fill All Cups)
"I Will Bring You Out"

Reader #2: The First Cup is the cup of sanctification and blessing, or as it was known anciently: "**I Will Bring You Out**," having reference to the promise of deliverance from Egypt.

Praise: "Blessed art thou, O Jehovah, our God, King of the Universe, Creator of the fruit of the vine. Blessed art thou, O Jehovah, our God, King of the Universe, who selected us from among all people and exalted us among nations, and did sanctify us with his commandments. And thou, O Jehovah, Our God, hast given us Sabbath days for rest and festival days for joy, this feast of the unleavened bread, the time of our deliverance in love in remembrance of the departure from Egypt. For us hast thou selected, and sanctified from amongst all nations, in that thou causedst us to inherit thy holy Sabbath and festival days in love and favour. Blessed art thou, O Eternal, who hallowest the Sabbath and Israel and the festival days."

All Drink From the Cup. Drink Completely.

Reader #3: Scriptural Commentary: "And [Jesus] took the cup, and gave thanks, and said, Take this, and divide it among yourselves: For I say unto you, I will not drink of the fruit of the vine, until the kingdom of God shall come" (Luke 22:17-18).

Commentary: Jesus' first recorded miracle is that of turning water to wine in Cana (John 2). People saw in this miracle fulfillment of ancient prophecy concerning the Messiah, that when He came, He would provide wine, milk and water in abundance. "And it shall come to pass in that day, that the mountains shall drop down new wine, and the hills shall flow with milk, and all the rivers of Judah shall flow with waters, and a fountain shall come forth of the house of the LORD, and shall water the valley of Shittim" (Joel 3:18).

This cup celebrates the promise of Jehovah to bring His people out of Egypt. Jesus invites His followers to come out of the spiritual wasteland, and into the Kingdom of God, where they will be equal heirs with Him.

Washing of Hands

Reader #4: "The earth is the LORD's, and the fulness thereof; the world, and they that dwell therein.

"For he hath founded it upon the seas, and established it upon the floods.

"Who shall ascend into the hill of the LORD?

"Or who shall stand in his holy place?

"He that hath clean hands, and a pure heart, who hath not lifted up his soul unto vanity nor sworn deceitfully.

"He shall receive the blessing from the LORD, and righteousness from the God of his salvation.

"This is the generation of them that seek him, that seek thy face, even Jacob."(Psalm 24:1-6).

Let us wash our hands. As we wash, let us renew our commitment to God to have 'clean hands and a pure heart.'

Instructions: A bowl is provided for you to dip your fingers in. Please do so now. With a small group, a pitcher would be used to pour water over the hands into a bowl.

Reader #5: Scholars are not in agreement as to when Jesus washed the feet of His disciples. Many feel that it would be at this point of the Feast that Jesus rose, girded Himself, and washed His disciples. His act would have been a sign of great love, even an act of servitude. This seems to be the natural point in the order of the

Passover ritual for Jesus to have performed the service, for we know that He washed Judas' feet, and that Judas left early in the evening.

Reader #6: Scriptural Commentary: "He riseth from supper, and laid aside his garments; and took a towel, and girded himself. After that he poureth water into a basin, and began to wash the disciples' feet, and to wipe them with the towel wherewith he was girded.

"Then cometh he to Simon Peter: and Peter saith unto him, Lord, dost thou wash my feet? Jesus answered and said unto him, What I do thou knowest not now; but thou shalt know hereafter. Peter saith unto him, Thou shalt never wash my feet. Jesus answered him, If I wash thee not, thou hast no part with me. Simon Peter saith unto him, Lord, not my feet only, but also my hands and my head.

"Jesus saith to him, He that is washed needeth not save to wash his feet, but is clean every whit: and ye are clean, but not all. For he knew who should betray him; therefore said he, Ye are not all clean" (John 13:4-11).

Karpas (Parsley in Saltwater)

Reader #7: We will take the parsley, called *kar-pas* and we will dip it into the salt water. We do this to symbolize the tears and pain of the Israelites. After the following prayer, take the parsley and dip it into the salt water and remember that even though we have painful circumstances in our lives, we will always have the hope of God to free us from our tribulations.

Praise: "Blessed art thou, O Eternal, our God, King of the Universe, Creator of the fruits of the earth."

Instructions: The reader breaks off parsley, dips in saltwater and eats it. All do the same.

Reader #8: The parsley represents fruitfulness of hope that God remembers His people. The saltwater represents the tears of His people.

Scriptural Commentary: "He will swallow up death in victory; and the Lord GOD will wipe away tears from off all faces; and the rebuke of his people shall he take away from off all the earth: for the LORD hath spoken it" (Isaiah 25:8).

"For the Lamb which is in the midst of the throne shall feed them, and shall lead them unto living fountains of waters: and God shall wipe away all tears from their eyes" (Revelation 7:17).

"And God shall wipe away all tears from their eyes; and there shall be no more death, neither sorrow, nor crying, neither shall there be any more pain: for the former things are passed away" (Revelation 21:4).

Breaking The Matzah

Instruction: The person who will read next raises a plate made ready with three matzahs and white linens. Hold the plate for all to see the matzah bread.

Reader #9: The children of Israel were instructed to eat unleavened bread for the Passover feast, and for seven days following the Passover. The symbolism of leaven has already been discussed. This bread represents purity, undefiled by worldly influence. It is beaten, pressed flat, bruised and pierced, as Jesus was also beaten, pressed in the "Olive Press" of the Garden in the Gethsemane, bruised and pierced.

Scriptural Commentary: "He is despised and rejected of men; a man of sorrows, and acquainted with grief: and we hid as it were our faces from him; he was despised, and we esteemed him not. Surely he hath borne our griefs, and carried our sorrows: yet we did esteem him stricken, smitten of God, and afflicted. But he was wounded for our transgressions, he was bruised for our iniquities; the chastisement of our peace was upon him; and with his stripes we are healed" (Isaiah 53:3-5).

"And I will pour upon the house of David, and upon the inhabitants of Jerusalem, the spirit of grace and of supplications: and they shall look upon me whom they have pierced, and they shall mourn for him, as one mourneth for his only son, and shall be in bitterness for him, as one that is in bitterness for his firstborn" (Zechariah 12:10).

Instructions: The reader takes the center matzah, and breaks it in two. One of the halves is hidden in a white napkin, to be "discovered" later. The other half is placed between the two whole pieces, wrapping a white napkin between each piece.

Reader #10: Some Rabbis say that the three pieces represent the High Priest, the Levites, and the People of Israel (the three forms of worship in temple times). But if this is so, why is the middle broken? Others say that the three pieces represent Abraham, Isaac, and Jacob. But this, too, does not explain why the middle matzah is broken. What, then, if each of the pieces of bread represent a member of the Godhead: Father, Son and Holy Ghost? The broken piece is to be "discovered" later in the Feast. Jesus was "broken" for His people, but many still do not recognize this. However, upon "discovering" Jesus, one may become whole, and come into a relationship of unity with each of the members of the Godhead.

ALL Speak: This is the bread of affliction which our ancestors ate in the land of Egypt; let all those who are hungry, enter and eat thereof; and all who are in distress, come and celebrate the Passover.

The Second Cup — Fill All Cups

"I Will Deliver You"

Instructions: Remember, do not drink until instructed to do so!

The Four Questions:

Reader#11: The Lord instructed the Children of Israel that they were to teach their "sons" to keep the Passover, and to tutor them in its meaning (Exodus 13:8). At this point in the Feast, four questions are asked, usually by the youngest child present. Many believe that this part of the Passover would have been spoken by John, who was the youngest of the Twelve present with Jesus.

Reader #12: Wherefore is this night distinguished from all other nights?

1) On All other nights we may eat either leavened or unleavened bread; but on this night why only unleavened bread?

2) On all other nights we may eat herbs of any kind; but on this night why only bitter herbs?

3) On all other nights we do not dip our herbs even once; but on this night why do we dip them twice?

4) On all other nights we eat our meals sitting or reclining; but on this night why do we eat in a reclining position?

ALL Speak: Because we were slaves unto Pharaoh in Egypt, and Jehovah, our God, brought us forth thence with a mighty hand and an outstretched arm. And if the Most Holy, blessed be He, had not brought forth our ancestors from Egypt, we and our children and our children's children would still be in bondage to the Pharaohs in Egypt. We therefore consider it a sacred duty and obligation to keep this miracle of salvation ever alive in our memories.

Reader #13: 1) We eat unleavened bread because when our ancestors were told by Pharaoh that they could leave Egypt, they had no time to bake bread with leaven, so they baked it without leaven.

2) At the Feast, we eat bitter herbs to remind us of the bitterness our ancestors experienced when they were oppressed by the Egyptian taskmasters.

3) At the Feast, we dip food twice: the parsley in salt water, as we have already explained, and the matzah into bitter herbs, as we shall later explain.

4) As a sign of freedom, we lean to the left when we partake of the cup. In ancient times, slaves ate hurriedly, standing, while royalty, and the wealthy in Egypt, and other empires, dined on couches. To show that Israel was now free, they too reclined while eating.

Reader #14: Commentary: Imagine John's asking the question: "What distinguishes this night from all other nights?" We could ask further, "What distinguished *that* Passover from all other Passovers? It was *the* night, *the* Passover, when the Lamb of God would give His life for a ransom for His people, that death would have no longer have power over them.

Reader #15: Following the four questions, are questions asked by four "sons" who represent varying levels of spiritual maturity: a wise one, a wicked one, a simple one, and one who is unable to ask for himself. Not all are equally equipped to receive the message of Passover; not all are equally sensitive to its importance. The questions they ask about the meaning of Passover and its rituals are different and varied, and must be responded to at the level of their understanding.

Recitation of the Passover Story

Reader #16: The Israelites were already in the land of Egypt. They became fertile and multiplied and increased very greatly, so that the land was filled with them. A new king arose over Egypt, who did not know Joseph, and imposed great labor and hardship on the Israelites. But the more the Israelites were oppressed, the more they increased. The king then ordered that all newborn baby boys be killed.

A Levite woman conceived and bore a son and hid him for three months. After that time, she prepared a wicker basket and laid the child in the basket and placed it among the reeds by the bank of the Nile. The daughter of Pharaoh came down to bathe in the Nile and saw the basket among the reeds and had her slave girl fetch the basket. The Pharaoh's daughter took pity on the child and made him her own son. She named him Moses, explaining, "I drew him out of water."

Reader #17: Moses grew and learned of his heritage. After witnessing an Egyptian beating an Israelite, he struck down the Egyptian and hid him in the sand. When Pharaoh learned of the matter, he sought to kill Moses, but Moses flew from Pharaoh. He arrived in the land of Midian, where he married his wife, Zipporah.

A long time had gone by and the king of Egypt died. The Israelites were groaning under bondage and cried out to God. God heard their cries. God appeared to Moses in a burning bush telling him that he would use Moses to lead His people out of Egypt into a land "flowing with milk and honey." So Moses returned to Egypt and Moses took the rod of God with him.

Moses and his brother Aaron went to the Pharaoh to ask for the release of their people. But the Pharaoh's heart was hardened against the Israelites and would not release them from the bondage of slavery. Each time the Pharaoh refused to let the Israelites go, the land of Egypt came under a great plague. With the tenth and most awful plague, the heart of Pharaoh would be pierced.

ALL Speak: "For I will pass through the land of Egypt this night, and will smite all the firstborn in the land of Egypt, both man and beast; and against all the gods of Egypt I will execute judgment: I am the LORD" (Exodus 12:12).

Reader #18: "And the blood [of the lamb] shall be to you for a token upon the houses where ye are: and when I see the blood, I will pass over you, and the plague shall not be upon you to destroy you, when I smite the land of Egypt" (Exodus 12:13).

"And this day shall be unto you for a memorial; and ye shall keep it a feast to the LORD throughout your generations; ye shall keep it a feast by an ordinance forever" (Exodus 12:14).

ALL Speak: By the blood of the lamb was Israel spared. By the blood of the lamb was Jacob redeemed. By the blood of the lamb was death made to pass over.

Reader #19: Scriptural Commentary: "He was oppressed, and he was afflicted, yet he opened not his mouth: he is brought as a lamb to the slaughter, and as a sheep before her shearers is dumb, so he openeth not his mouth" (Isaiah 53:7).

ALL Speak: And we cried unto the Eternal, the God of our fathers, and the Eternal heard our voice, saw our affliction, our sorrow, and our oppression. And the Eternal brought us forth from Egypt, with a strong hand and with an outstretched arm, with great terror, and with signs and wonders. And the Eternal brought us forth from Egypt: not by means of an angel, nor by means of a Seraph, nor by means of a messenger; but the most Holy, blessed be He, in His own glory.

Reader #20: Just as the blood of those first Passover lambs was applied in faith to the doorposts of Israel's homes, so the blood of the Messiah must be applied in faith to the doorposts of our hearts.

Scriptural Commentary: "Then said Jesus unto them again, verily, verily, I say unto you, I am the door of the sheep. … I am the door: by me if any man enter in, he shall be saved, and shall go in and out and find pasture" (John 10:7,9).

"O then, my beloved brethren, come unto the Lord the Holy One. Remember his paths are righteous. Behold, the way for man is narrow, but it lieth in a straight course before him, and the keeper of the gate is the Holy One of Israel; and he employeth no servant there; and there is none other way save it be by the gate; for he cannot be deceived for the Lord God is his name" (2 Nephi 9:41).

Reader #21: "And one of the elders saith unto me, Weep not: behold the Lion of the tribe of Judah, the Root of David, hath prevailed to open the book, and to loose the seven seals thereof. And I beheld, and, lo, in the midst of the throne and of the four beats, and in the midst of the elders, stood a Lamb as it had been slain …" (Revelation 5:5-6).

Reader #22: A "Recitation of the Plagues" occurs at this point of the Feast. Often, this is done in a spirit of fun and frivolity, but in keeping with a remembrance of the Savior's last Passover, it can be acknowledged in context with the "three symbols," following.

The Three Symbols

Reader #23: This Paschal lamb, which our ancestors ate during the existence of the temple – for what reason was it eaten? Because the Holy One, blessed be He, passed over the houses of our ancestors in Egypt, as it is said: "Ye shall say, it is a sacrifice of the Passover unto the Lord, who passed over the houses of the children of Israel in Egypt."

Commentary: "The ordinary evening service and sacrifice in the temple must precede the supper. On this feast day this service began an hour early, or at about 1:30 PM, with the evening sacrifice itself being offered at about 2:30 PM. This was the time for the slaying of the Paschal lambs by their owners and the sprinkling of their blood upon the altar by the priests. Both Mark and Luke say that Peter and John were to 'make ready' the Passover meal, and they both record that 'they made ready the passover.' Of necessity this means that the two apostles, rather than the homeowner or some other person, were required to, and did attend the temple services for the formal slaying and preparation of the lamb; and to this assumption there is a certain fitness and propriety: two of the chief apostles, for themselves and on behalf of their Lord and their brethren, were complying to the full to the letter of the law on the last day on which its provisions were in force. When, on the morrow, the true Paschal Lamb was slain, the old order would be over and the new covenant only would have binding efficacy and force" (McConkie, Mortal Messiah, 4:25).

"It was done on this wise: The first of the three festive divisions, with their Paschal lambs, was admitted within the court of the Priests. Each division must consist of not less than thirty persons (3 X 10, the symbolic number of the Divine and of completeness). Immediately the massive gates were closed behind them. The priests drew a threefold blast from their silver trumpets when the Passover was slain. Altogether the scene was most impressive. All along the Court up to the altar of burnt-offering priests stood in two rows, the one holding golden, the other silver bowls. In these the blood of the Paschal lambs, which each Israelite slew for himself (as representative of his company at the Paschal Suppers), was caught up by a priest, who handed it to his colleague, receiving back an empty bowl, and so the bowls with the blood were passed up to the priest at the altar, who jerked it in one jet at the base of the altar. While this was going on, a most solemn 'hymn' of praise was raised, the Levites leading in song, and the offerers either repeating after them or merely responding. This service of song consisted of the so-called 'Hallel,' which comprised Psalm 113 to 118, working its way to the crescendo for the phrases: 'Save now, I beseech thee, O LORD: O LORD, I beseech thee, send now prosperity. Blessed be he that cometh in the name of the LORD: we have blessed you out of the house of the LORD'" (Edersheim, The Temple: Its Ministry and Services, pp. 175-76).

Reader #24: The unleavened bread which we now eat, what does it mean? It is eaten because the dough of our ancestors had not time to become leavened, before the supreme King of kings, the Most Holy, blessed be He! revealed Himself unto them, and they baked unleavened cakes of the dough which they had brought forth out of Egypt, for it was not leavened, because they were thrust out of Egypt, and could not tarry, neither had they made any provision for themselves.

Commentary: The unleavened bread represents the bricks the Israelites were forced to make in Egypt. Leaving out the leaven from the bread represents removing the spoiling influences of the world. It also reminds the children of Israel that they had to leave Egypt in a hurry. We must cleanse the impurities of the world from our lives, and there is urgency in the commandment to do so.

Reader #25: This bitter herb which we eat, what does it mean? It is eaten because the Egyptians embittered the lives of our ancestors in Egypt. The bitterness of sin is the worst form of slavery.

Scriptural Commentary: "Behold, for peace I had great bitterness: but thou hast in love to my soul delivered it from the pit of corruption: for thou hast cast all my sins behind thy back" (Isaiah 38:17).

"My soul hath been redeemed from the gall of bitterness and bonds of iniquity. I was in the darkest abyss; but now I behold the marvelous light of God. My soul was racked with eternal torment, but I am snatched, and my soul is pained no more" (Mosiah 27:29).

Instructions: All Raise the Second Cup – But do not drink!

Reader #26: Praise ye the LORD. Praise, O ye servants of the LORD, praise the name of the LORD.

Blessed be the name of the LORD from this time forth and for evermore.

From the rising of the sun unto the going down of the same the LORD's name is to be praised.

The LORD is high above all nations, and his glory above the heavens.

Who is like unto the LORD our God, who dwelleth on high,

Who humbleth himself to behold the things that are in heaven, and in the earth!

He raiseth up the poor out of the dust, and lifteth the needy out of the dunghill;

That he may set him with princes, even with the princes of his people.

He maketh the barren woman to keep house, and to be a joyful mother of children.

Praise ye the LORD.

Reader #27: When Israel went out of Egypt, the house of Jacob from a people of strange language;

Judah was his sanctuary, and Israel his dominion.

The sea saw it, and fled: Jordan was driven back.

The mountains skipped like rams, and the little hills like lambs.

What ailed thee, O thou sea, that thou fleddest?

Thou Jordan, that thou wast driven back?

Ye mountains, that ye skipped like rams; and ye little hills, like lambs?

Tremble, thou earth, at the presence of the Lord, at the presence of the God of Jacob;

Which turned the rock into a standing water, the flint into a fountain of waters.

ALL Speak: Blessed art thou, Jehovah, our God, King of the Universe, who hast redeemed us. We give thanks to Thee for our deliverance and for the redemption of our souls. Blessed art thou, O Jehovah, who hast redeemed Israel.

Instructions: All drink of the Second Cup: "I Will Deliver You."

Second Hand Washing Preparatory to Meal

Instructions: All dip fingers in bowls.

Blessing of the Bread

Reader #28: Blessed art thou, O Lord our God, King of the Universe, who bringest forth bread from the earth.

Instruction: Break bread and distribute.

Show the bitter herbs to the assembly. Show the Charoseth, or Maror (apple mixture) to the assembly. "The Charoseth represents the Egyptian mortar. Take the bread, dip it in the bitter herbs and the Charoseth, and eat it, that the scripture may be fulfilled which says: 'They shall eat it [the Passover offering] with matzah and bitter herbs" (Exodus 12:8).

Reader #29: Commentary: "This sandwich was eaten with lamb during temple times in Jerusalem, it is also known as the sop. It is still the custom today to give this dipped sop with affection to a loved one.

"This, in all probability, was 'the sop' which, in answer to John's inquiry about the betrayer, the Lord 'gave' to Judas" (Edersheim, *The Temple: Its Ministry and Services*, p. 190).

Scriptural Commentary: "I speak not of you all: I know whom I have chosen: but that the scripture may be fulfilled, He that eateth bread with me hath lifted up his heel against me. Now I tell you before it come, that, when it is come to pass, ye may believe that I am the Christ.

"When Jesus had thus said, he was troubled in spirit, and testified, and said, Verily, verily, I say unto you, that one of you shall betray me. Then the disciples looked one on another, doubting of whom he spake. Now there was leaning on Jesus' bosom one of his disciples, whom Jesus loved. Simon Peter therefore beckoned to him, that he should ask who it should be of whom he spake. He then lying on Jesus' breast saith unto him, Lord, who is it? Jesus answered, He it is, to whom I shall give a sop, when I have dipped it. And when he had dipped the sop, he gave it to Judas Iscariot, the son of Simon. And after the sop Satan entered into him. Then said Jesus unto him, That thou doest, do quickly" (John 13:18-27).

Blessing of the Lamb

Reader #30: The sacrifice of the lambs would take place in what we would consider a two-day period; but in actuality occurred in a 24-hour period the Jews referred to as "one day." The poorer people, who had fewer preparations to make for a feast, would begin their Passover feasts on what we would now call the first day. The priests, who had to officiate in the sacrifices, and the wealthier citizens of the community would finish their sacrifices by 2:30 of what we would call the second day, ending their duties, and partaking of the Feast before sundown. Thus, Jesus, the Lamb of God, hung on the cross at the time the priests were performing the sacrifices for their own tables; He having performed the atonement in Gethsemane the night before.

Eating of the Feast

Instructions: Prayer by invitation.

The Afikomen

The Hidden Bread

Reader #31: The broken matzah, called the *Afikomen*, hidden at the beginning of the meal must now be found by the children present at the feast. A reward is given to those who find it. The *Afikomen* is the final food of the Passover Feast, and is considered the dessert; the sweetest portion of the Feast.

Scriptural Commentary: "With my soul have I desired thee in the night; yea, with my spirit within me will I seek thee early: for when thy judgments are in the earth, the inhabitants of the world will learn righteousness" (Isaiah 26:9).

"Yet they seek me daily, and delight to know my ways, as a nation that did righteousness, and forsook not the ordinance of their God: they ask of me the ordinances of justice; they take delight in approaching to God" (Isaiah 58:2).

Reader #32: "And ye shall seek me, and find me, when ye shall search for me with all your heart" (Jeremiah 29:13).

"Draw near unto me and I will draw near unto you; seek me diligently and ye shall find me; ask, and ye shall receive, knock, and it shall be opened unto you" (D&C 88:63).

Question and Discussion: Why is it that the children are the ones who are to seek?

Reader #33: Scriptural Commentary: "And [He] said, Verily I say unto you, Except ye be converted, and become as little children, ye shall not enter into the kingdom of heaven" (Matthew 18:3).

"He that seeketh me early shall find me, and shall not be forsaken" (D&C 88:83).

Reader #34: Commentary: Though He was broken and buried, Jesus rose again, and "every knee shall bow, and every tongue confess" that Jesus is the Christ (Romans 14:11). Those who "find" the Lord find sweetness and satisfaction to their souls.

Reader #35: Scriptural Commentary: "And as they did eat, Jesus took bread and blessed it, and brake, and gave to them and said, Take it, and eat. Behold, this is for you to do in remembrance of my body; for as oft as ye do this ye will remember this hour that I was with you" (JST Mark 14:20-21).

"And Jesus said unto them, I am the bread of life: he that cometh to me shall never hunger; and he that believeth on me shall never thirst. I am that bread of life. I am the living bread which came down from heaven: if any man eat of this bread, he shall live forever: and the bread that I will give is my flesh, which I will give for the life of the world" (John 6:35, 48, 51).

Let us eat the bread as our *Afikomen*, the dessert that is sweet to the taste, remembering the gift of His own life that the Savior gave in our behalf. Its taste should linger in our mouths and hearts.

The Third Cup — (Fill All Cups)

"I Will Redeem You"

Instructions: Do not drink of the cup until instructed to do so.

Reader #36: While all commentators agree that this is the cup wherein Jesus instituted the sacrament, it is unknown precisely where in the lengthy oration for this cup He did so, or if they participated in the script at all. It has been placed by this author in context with the plea to behold the face of the Messiah. There is a possibility that the Savior simply filled and blessed the cup and proceeded with the sacramental instruction, bypassing the customary ritual. In any case, it is meaningful to read and ponder the traditional script.

Since Passover, the Festival of Freedom, expresses hope in the eventual redemption of mankind and its deliverance from all evil, who could be a more welcome guest at the Seder than Elijah? And so, in every Jewish home a special cup is reserved for the Prophet Elijah

The door to the house is now opened as a symbol of our belief that the coming of a Messianic Age is not an impossible dream. We, too, look for it, hope for it, pray for it, as have our ancestors for hundreds of generations before us.

ALL Speak: Elijah the Prophet,

Elijah the Tishbite,

Elijah, Elijah, Elijah the Gileadite!

May he soon come,

Soon in our day,

Ushering in the Messiah – son of David!

Reader #37: Scriptural Commentary: "Behold, I will send you Elijah the prophet before the coming of the great and dreadful day of the LORD: And he shall turn the hearts of the fathers to the children, and the heart of the children to their fathers, lest I come and smite the earth with a curse" (Malachi 4:5-6).

"April 3, 1836 (Passover), the following occurred in the Kirtland, Ohio, Temple: 'After this vision had closed another great and glorious vision burst upon us; for Elijah the prophet, who was taken to heaven without tasting death, stood before us, and said: Behold, the time has fully come, which was spoken of by the mouth of Malachi — testifying that he [Elijah] should be sent, before the great and dreadful day of the Lord come — To turn the hearts of the fathers to the children, and the children to the fathers, lest the whole earth be smitten with a curse — Therefore, the keys of this dispensation are committed into your hands; and by this ye may know that the great and dreadful day of the Lord is near, even at the doors" (D&C 110:13-16).

Reader #38: Our God, and the God of our fathers, Mayest thou be pleased to grant that our remembrance and the remembrance of our fathers, the remembrance of the Messiah, the son of David, thy servant, and the remembrance of Jerusalem, thy holy city, and the remembrance of thy people, the house of Israel may ascend, come, approach, be seen, accepted, heard and remembered for the granting of a happy deliverance, with favour, grace, mercy, life and peace on this day of Passover … And with the word of salvation and mercy, have compassion and be gracious unto us! O have mercy upon us and save us, for our eyes are continually toward thee, for thou, O Lord, art a merciful and gracious King.

At this point in the Passover Feast, the participants would ask that they might behold the day of the Messiah. "May

He who is most merciful, make us worthy to behold the day of the Messiah …

Reader #39: Scriptural Commentary: "And he took the cup, and when he had given thanks, he gave it to them; and they all drank of it. And he said unto them, This is in remembrance of my blood which is shed for many and the new testament which I give unto you; for of me ye shall bear record unto all the world. And as oft as ye do this ordinance, ye will remember me in this hour that I was with you and drank with you of this cup, even the last time in my ministry. Verily I say unto you, of this ye shall bear record; for I will no more drink of the fruit of the vine with you, until that day that I drink it new in the kingdom of God" (JST Mark 14:22-25).

"The cup of blessing which we bless, is it not the communion of the blood of Christ? The bread which we break, is it not the communion of the body of Christ? For we being many are one bread, and one body: for we are all partakers of that one bread" (1 Corinthians 10:16-17).

Instructions: All drink of the 3rd cup, not as the sacrament ordinance, but in remembrance of the sacrifice of Christ's blood; finding communion with one another and with Him, that we may all "be one" as He instructed.

The Fourth Cup — (Fill All Cups)
"I Will Take You To Me"

Instructions: Do not drink of the cup until instructed to do so.

Reader #40: The service concludes with the fourth cup, over which the second portion of the 'Hallel' was sung, consisting of Psalms 115-118, the whole ending with the so-called 'blessing of the song,' which comprised these two brief prayers:

ALL Speak: All Thy works shall praise Thee, Jehovah our God. And Thy saints, the righteous, who do Thy good pleasure, and all Thy people, the house of Israel, with joyous song let them praise, and bless, and magnify, and glorify, and exalt, and reverence, and sanctify, and ascribe the kingdom to Thy name, O our King! For it is good to praise Thee, and pleasure to sing praises unto Thy name, for from everlasting to everlasting Thou art God.

The breath of all that lives shall praise Thy name, Jehovah our God. And the spirit of all flesh shall continually glorify and exalt Thy memorial, O our King! For from everlasting to everlasting Thou art God, and besides Thee we have no King, Redeemer or Saviour.

Reader #41: "O give thanks unto the LORD; for he is good: because his mercy endureth for ever. Let Israel now say, that his mercy endureth for ever. Let the house of Aaron now say, that his mercy endureth for ever. Let them now that fear the LORD say, that his mercy endureth for ever.

"I called upon the LORD in distress: the LORD answered me, and set me in a large place. The LORD is on my side; I will not fear: what can man do unto me?

"The Lord is my strength and song, and is become my salvation. The voice of rejoicing and salvation is in the tabernacles of the righteous: the right hand of the LORD doeth valiantly. \I shall not die, but live, and declare the works of the LORD. The LORD hath chastened me sore: but he hath not given me over unto death.

"Open to me the gates of righteousness: I will go into them, and I will praise the LORD: This gate of the LORD, into which the righteous shall enter. I will praise thee: for thou hast heard me, and art become my salvation.

"The stone which the builders refused is become the head stone of the corner. This is the LORD's doing; it is marvelous in our eyes.

"This is the day which the LORD hath made; we will rejoice and be glad in it. Save now, I beseech thee, O LORD: O LORD, I beseech thee … Thou art my God, and I will praise thee: thou art my God, I will exalt thee. O give thanks unto the LORD; for he is good: for his mercy endureth forever" (Psalm 118: 1-6, 14-29).

All Drink of the Fourth Cup

The Feast Closes

Reader #42: Those who celebrate the Passover today have added the following: "In closing, we call out to our Lord and God, Have compassion, O Lord our God, upon us, upon Israel Your people, upon Jerusalem Your city, on Zion the dwelling place of Your glory, and upon Your altar and Your Temple. Rebuild Jerusalem, Your holy city, speedily in our days. Be gracious to us and give us strength.

O Pure One in heaven above, restore the congregation of Israel in Your love, speedily lead Your redeemed people to Zion in joy.

ALL Speak: Next year in Jerusalem!

Reader #43: "Behold, the days come, saith the LORD, that I will make a new covenant with the house of Israel, and with the house of Judah: Not according to the covenant that I made with their fathers in the day that I took them by the hand to bring them out of the land of Egypt, which my covenant they brake, although I was an husband unto them, saith the

LORD: But this shall be the covenant that I will make with the house of Israel; After those days, saith the LORD, I will put my law in their inward parts, and write it in their hearts; and will be their God, and they shall be my people. And they shall teach no more every man his neighbor, and every man his brother, saying, Know the LORD: for they shall all know me, from the least of them unto the greatest of them, saith the LORD: for I will forgive their iniquity, and I will remember their sin no more" (Jeremiah 31:31-34).

Jesus And His Apostles

Reader #44: Jesus said, "A new commandment I give unto you, That ye love one another; as I have loved you, that ye also love one another. By this shall all men know that ye are my disciples, if ye have love one to another" (John 13:34-35).

Reader #45: The word "love" is used 26 times in John, chapters 13-15, which records this great Passover event. John had had the role of the youngest, who asks: "What distinguishes this night from all other nights?" This night is distinguished by love. As John wrote: "We love Him because He first loved us" (1 John 4:19).

As their Supper ended, they sang a song, and Jesus, Peter, James and John left for the Garden of Gethsemane. There, Jesus would drink a bitter cup, and drain it to its dregs.

All Sing "As I Have Loved You."

Closing Prayer: By Invitation